Write Your Own
Fantasy Stories

Tish Farrell

Your writing quest

Enchanted lands with wizards and elves, parallel realms of hero mice and roving dragons – do magic worlds like this capture your imagination? Then learn how to transform your own story ideas into fantastic tales. This book won't give you any magic spells, but it will help you on your quest to become a good fantasy writer.

Your first challenge is to discover the Lost Mines of Your Imagination – set free the stories that are held captive there. This won't always be easy. You will encounter many blocks and obstacles, but if you follow the advice and exercises in this book, you will gain all the special skills you need to reach your goal. To help you, there will be tips and guidance from some famous writers, and examples from their books to give you more ideas.

But don't forget! Becoming a good writer takes time and practice. Like all fine quests, there are few short cuts.

Now, get ready for some story 'conjuring'.

Good luck!

Copyright © ticktock Entertainment Ltd 2007
First published in Great Britain in 2006 by ticktock Media Ltd.,
Unit 2, Orchard Business Centre, North Farm Road, Tunbridge Wells, Kent, TN2 3XF
ISBN 1 86007 924 5 PB
Printed in China 10 9 8 7 6 5 4 3 2
A CIP catalogue record for this book is available from the British Library.

CONTENTS

WANT TO BE A WRITER?

This book aims to give you the tools to write your own fantasy fiction. Learn how to craft believable characters, perfect plots, and satisfying beginnings, middles and endings.

Step-by-step instruction

The pages throughout the book include numbers providing step-by-step instructions or a series of options that will help you to master certain parts of the writing process. To create beginnings, middles and ends, for example, complete 18 simple steps.

Chronological progress

You can follow your progress by using the bar located on the bottom of each page. The orange colour tells you how far along the story-writing process you have got. As the blocks are filled out, so your story will be gathering pace...

---

44 CHAPTER 7: SCINTILLATING SPEECH

CREATING DIALOGUE

Dialogue is your big chance to bring your creations to life. Your readers can 'hear' your characters' own voices and it also helps to break up a page of narrative (storytelling) giving readers' eyes a rest. It is a powerful storytelling tool – one that can add colour, pace, mood and suspense to your story.

❶ Let your characters speak for themselves

The best way to learn about dialogue is to switch on your listening ear and eavesdrop. Tune into the way people phrase their words. Write down any good idioms – someone saying 'sling your hook' or 'shove off' instead of 'go away'. Watch people's body language too when they are whispering or arguing. Look, listen and absorb...

TIPS AND TECHNIQUES

When writing dialogue, don't just stick to 'he said/she said' all the time. Use words like 'asked', 'replied', 'exclaimed', 'cried', 'whispered', etc. to create excitement and variety in your writing.

GETTING STARTED	WRITING STYLES AND IDEAS	CREATING CHARACTERS	VIEWPOI

Each section explains a key part of the writing process, from creating believable landscapes and characters to structuring a story itself. Once you have got to the end of the bar, you story is ready! *Write Your Own...* ends with looking at the next step - what do you want to do next? Write a sequel? Tell a story from the viewpoint of another character in the first story? Or perhaps try something completely different...

Box features

Appearing throughout the book, these four different colour-coded box types help you with the writing process by providing inspiration, examples from other books, background details and hints and tips.

❷ Following convention

he way dialogue is written down follows conventions
r rules too. It is usual to start a new paragraph with
very new speaker. What they say is enclosed in single
r double inverted commas, followed by 'he said' or
he said' to indicate the speaker. Other information
ay be added, such as the speaker's feelings or actions.
ee too, how inserting tags in the middle of some
peech lines, gives the impression of a real conversation
reading aloud, this actually creates a rhythmic flow
at makes the exchanges easier to follow.

Case study

As a child, Kate DiCamillo suffered from chronic pneumonia, and entertained herself by reading. When she was in her twenties, she discovered a new love for children's books, and began writing her own. Perhaps because of her background, dialogue is very important in her books. She describes **Because of Winn-Dixie** as "a hymn to dogs, friendship, and the South."

"Would it be possible for me to have a last word with the princess?" Despereaux asked. "A word?" said the second hood. "You want a word with a human?" "I want to tell her what happened to me." "Geez," said the first hood. He stopped and stamped a paw on the floor in frustration. "Cripes. You can't learn can you."

Kate DiCamillo (right), *The Tale of Despereaux*

Now it's your turn

Writing a good argument

Remember an argument you had or heard. Fictionalise it, change the names but pour anger into the words. Don't rely on tags like 'yelled' or 'screamed' to show the mood. Think too: the speakers are trying to hurt each other! Their words will fire off like bullets or build quietly to a fatal blow depending on their character. When you have finished, read it aloud. Now revise it. Take out any unnecessary 'saids'. Cut down all the spoken words to the bare bones, then read it aloud once more. You are learning another absolutely essential writing skill – the art of editing your own work.

PSES & PLOTS | WINNING WORDS | SCINTILLATING SPEECH | HINTS & TIPS | FINISHING TOUCHES | WHAT NEXT!

Case study boxes

These boxes provide history on famous fantasy writers - what inspired them, how they started and more details.

Quote boxes

Turn to these green boxes to find quotes taken from published fantasy books by famous authors such as J.K. Rowling and Philip Pullman.

Now it's your turn boxes

These boxes provide a chance for you to put into practise what you have just been reading about. Simple, useful and fun exercises to help you build your writing skills.

Tips and techniques boxes

These boxes provide writing tips that will help you when you get stuck, or provided added inspiration to get to the next level.

WHY DO WRITERS WRITE?

No writer would say that writing is easy. Most well-known writers will have toiled for years before seeing their first stories in print. They write to tell a story that must be told and because they believe that nothing is more important than stories.

Brian Jacques

Brian Jacques (below right) wrote his first story at the age of ten. His teacher said it was so good that he couldn't possibly have written it. He left school at fifteen and did many jobs, but it was when he was a milkman that he wrote his first Redwall story to read out to the children there. His old English teacher secretly sent a copy of this story off to a publisher, and that is how he won a contract to write the first five books in the Tales of *Redwall* series. His advice: *Remember that television can't take you places the way that books can. So read, read, read.*

Christopher Paolini

Christopher Paolini was still a teenager when his first book *Eragon* was published to much acclaim. He says writers need to write about what excites them most, or they won't have the enthusiasm to write a whole novel – *be persistent; be disciplined; be humble enough to accept editorial criticism; learn everything you can about the writer's craft.*

J. K. Rowling

JK Rowling (left) wrote her first story when she was five or six. It was about a rabbit called Rabbit, and from then on, she knew she only wanted to be a writer. All the same, it was only when she was grown up and bringing up her own small daughter that she finally finished her first *Harry Potter* novel. It took her five years to write. This wasn't her first book either. She had already written and put aside two novels for adults. Rowling says that *being able to say I was a published author was the fulfilment of a dream.*

Philip Pullman

Pullman (right) goes to his desk every day at 9.30 a.m. and works until lunch time. He writes by hand and aims to write three sides of A4 paper. If he reaches this target, he spends the afternoon woodworking or playing the piano. If he hasn't, he goes back to his desk until he has. He always finishes his last sentence, or writes a new one, at the top of the fourth sheet – so he won't be faced with a blank page when he starts work the next day. He says that *a lot of the time you're going to be writing without inspiration. The trick is to write just as well without it as with it.*

FIRST THINGS FIRST

First gather your writing materials and find your story-making place. One of the best things about being a writer is that you don't need much equipment. Fantasy writers need only pen and paper or a computer to make their magic.

❶ Gather your writing materials

Apart from a pen and paper, you may also need to use your library and the Internet for research. As you learn your craft, it's also handy to have the following:

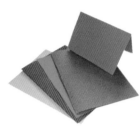

- Small notebook that you carry everywhere
- Coloured pencils (think magic wands!) to create your fantasy world
- Pens with gold and silver ink to record magical thoughts

- Different coloured post-it notes to mark any important book passages or keep track of ideas
- Stick-on stars to highlight your best ideas
- Files and folders to keep precious story ideas safe
- Dictionary, thesaurus and encyclopedia.

❷ Find a writing place

Writers can work wherever they like. Roald Dahl (*The BFG*) and Philip Pullman (*His Dark Materials* trilogy) wrote in their garden sheds. J. K. Rowling (*Harry Potter* series) wrote in a cafe. You may find your bedroom is the best place, or a quiet corner of the library. Experiment. See where you feel most comfortable, but wherever it is, sit up straight – hunched-up writers block the flow of oxygen to their brains, which makes for lacklustre tales.

❸ Create a writing zone

- Play music to encourage magical thoughts
- Spray an unusual spicy scent
- Spread out a selection of fantasy pictures
- Put on a writing hat (make your own or adapt one)

- Choose some mysterious objects for your writing space – interesting things you've collected from the beach, a quartz crystal, a pure white feather…Things that have a story to tell.

TIPS AND TECHNIQUES

Once you have found your writing place, the golden rule of becoming a real writer is: Go there as often as possible, and write something! This is called the writer's golden rule.

❹ Get in training

Before you can conjure duels with dragons (left) or challenge evil magicians, you must get into training. It may sound dull, but it has to be done. The best writers practise writing every day, even when they haven't got a story to tell, or don't feel at all inspired. You need to exercise your writing 'muscles' in the same way you would train to play football or practise the piano before a performance.

❺ Brainstorming

If writers get stuck, they can sometimes solve the problem using exciting sentences to spark off ideas. For example:

• *The day it rained broomsticks*
• *How I turned my gerbil/cat/labrador into a handsome prince and the terrible trouble it caused my family.*

Brainstorming with a friend can be fun. You may come up with ideas as a team that might never have occurred to you on your own.

TIPS AND TECHNIQUES

Make a regular date with your writing desk. Your practice may be five minutes or an hour. The trick is to stick to it.

Now it's your turn

Learn to unlock your imagination

Decide in advance how long your first writing practice will be.
It could be two minutes to begin with. Now close your eyes and take
four slow deep breaths. Open your eyes, check the time and write
the phrase 'Sword in the Stone' (right) at the top of the page.
Then BRAINSTORM! See how many other magical words,
names and phrases you can think of. Write everything that
comes into your head. Don't take your pen from the paper.
SPLURGE like troll vomit! Stop when
your two minutes are up.
Hurray! You've proved
you can write.

❻ Reward yourself!

When you've finished the task above, give yourself a gold star.
You are on your way to finding the *Lost Mines of Your
Imagination.* The more you do exercises like this, the easier
it will be to overcome the writer's worst enemy – the Story
Spectre. The voice in your head that continually picks fault
with your writing, which is also called your internal critic.

Case study

*Eoin Colfer used to be a teacher. Every afternoon after
school, and before looking after his little boy, he would
grab an hour to work on
his first book, the best-
selling Artemis Fowl.*

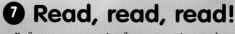

❼ Read, read, read!

Before you can write fantasy stories, such as the *Harry Potter* series (left), you need to know what it is. Fantasy is a genre that often sets its stories in imagined worlds, ruled by magic – usually with wizards or witches who know how to use it. But the magic always has some limitations. Begin by reading as many different fantasy stories as you can find. If something sparks your imagination write it down in a notebook.

❽ Discover your tastes

Think more deeply about the books you like. Are they set in totally different worlds with wizards and magic forces, like J. R. R. Tolkien's *The Lord of the Rings (right)*? Or do you like the story to move back and forth between real and imagined places as in C. S. Lewis's *The Chronicles of Narnia?* Or do you prefer something comic, set in the real world, such as Roald Dahl's *Matilda?*

❾ Look more deeply

Go back to a favourite fantasy story and, as you read, imagine that you are writing it. Start looking for the things that make that world so believable. When you first read it you probably completely lost yourself in it, and forgot all about the real world.

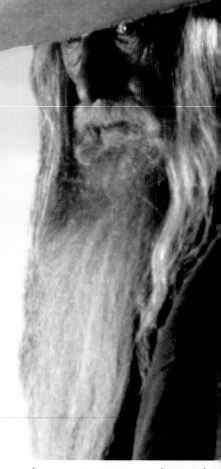

⑩ Inspiration from myths and legends

Have you noticed how fantasy stories draw their ideas from other stories? *The Wizard of Oz* (right), *The Hobbit, The BFG, His Dark Materials* trilogy – all have their roots in ancient myths and fairy tales. Tolkien may have had Merlin in mind when he created Gandalf.

⑪ Create illusions

As a trainee writer, you want to discover why and how stories work. This is rather like trying to spot how a magician performs his tricks. Story writing is all about creating illusions. So, as you study your best-loved stories, look for the particular things that made you think that somewhere, in some other place, space or time, the magic worlds described in them really did exist.

TIPS AND TECHNIQUES

As you read, think about whose story you want to tell. What kind of world do they live in? Write everything down in your notebook and, when you come to write your story, you will have plenty of characters and places to choose from. If you're not enjoying a book, leave it and start one that does grab you. Keep inspired and the ideas will flow...

A WRITER'S VOICE

To become a good writer it also helps to read as much as you can. This is the only way you'll discover your own writer's voice – a style of writing uniquely yours. This is something that takes time to develop.

❶ Finding your voice

Once you start reading with your writer's mind switched on, you will notice that writers have their own rhythm, style and range of language that stays the same throughout the book. Philip Pullman, author of *Northern Lights*, would never write like Lemony Snicket, author of *A Series of Unfortunate Events*. *Harry Potter* creator J. K. Rowling's voice is nothing like *Artemis Fowl* author Eoin Colfer's even though they both write humourously.

❷ Experiment

Once you've found an author whose books you really enjoy, it's tempting to stick to them. Don't! Experiment. Once in a while read something quite different: a historical novel or a book of legends. You may be surprised what ideas it gives you.

Case study

Eoin Colfer (above) drew inspiration for *Artemis Fowl* from Irish history and the wealth of traditional Irish legends.

WRITERS' VOICES

Look at the kinds of words these authors use. Do they use lots of adjectives? What about the length of their sentences? Which style do you prefer to read?

HANS CHRISTIAN ANDERSEN

The snow-flake grew bigger and bigger, until at last it turned into a lady clothed in the finest white gauze made up of millions of star-like snow-flakes. She was very beautiful, but she was of ice, dazzling, gleaming ice, all through, and yet she was alive.

Hans Christian Andersen, *The Snow Queen*

EOIN COLFER

Commander Root was sucking on a particularly noxious fungus cigar. Several of the Retrieval Squad had nearly passed out... Even the pong from the manacled troll seemed mild in comparison.

Eoin Colfer, *Artemis Fowl*

PHILIP PULLMAN

A cold drench of terror went down Lyra's spine... She had one day in which to find Roger and discover whatever she could about this place, and either escape or be rescued; and if all the gyptians had been killed, who would help the children stay alive in the icy wilderness?

Philip Pullman, *Northern Lights*

KATE DiCAMILLO

In the dungeon, there were rats. Large rats. Mean rats. Despereaux was destined to meet those rats. Reader, you must know that an interesting fate awaits almost everyone, mouse or man, who does not conform.

Kate DiCamillo, *The Tale of Despereaux*

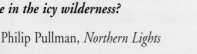

❸ Don't panic!

If you are stuck for story ideas, don't panic! That will just make your brain go blank. In fact, you already have lots of ideas, locked away in the *Lost Mines of Your Imagination*. This is where your subconscious memory stores every story experience you ever had.

❹ Freeing your stories

The true writer's art is to extract all the brilliant story strands that are hidden in his or her head and shape them into sparkling new tales. Brainstorming is a good way to start accessing your subconscious memory, but you'll probably need some extra tricks, too, before you can free your stories.

❺ Idea search

If you ask writers where they get their ideas they will say things like 'everywhere', or a character 'just came to them'. In fact, most writers such as Charles Dickens (left) store ideas for years, gathering information both consciously and subconsciously. Things get mixed up with memories and other stories and conversations they overhear. People they meet get mixed in too, along with newspaper articles, song lyrics, bits of poems. Everyone does this, but writers do it on purpose. Once in a while, something triggers a fully formed character or story.

Case study

Philip Pullman says he's stolen ideas from every book he's read. By this, he doesn't mean that he's copied what other writers have written. He means that his own story ideas are often inspired by memories of the things he has read: from comics to poetry to ancient stories.

Now it's your turn

Brainstorming

Speed up your ideas search with this brainstorming
exercise. Cut up some scrap paper into ten squares (big
enough to write one name on). Do the same with five
different coloured
sheets of paper, so
you end up with six piles
of ten squares. Now you are going to write,
as fast as you can, the first thoughts that come
into your mind. On your first pile of squares,
write the names of ten possible heroes
(or protagonists), one per square (e.g.
Witchfinder-Elfgirl). The other piles are for:
the main villain (or antagonist) (e.g. Worst
Witch); a name for your fantasy world or a
part of it (e.g. Heights of Horus); a magical
object that will be important in the story
(e.g. Truth Wand), a hero's helper (e.g. Silver
Falcon), and a villain's henchman (e.g. Man-eating Cat).

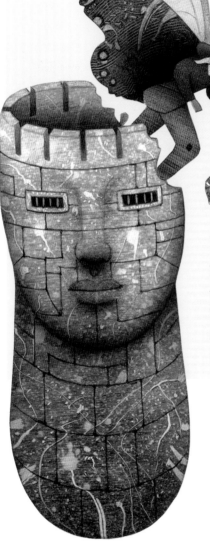

Now shuffle each pile and place them face down on your
writing desk. Turn over the top square from each pile.
There! You now have six vital ingredients for a fantasy
story: heroes, villains, a place, and an object for them
to battle over.

TIPS AND TECHNIQUES

*Keep your brainstorming notes in your notebook or in
a separate file. A lot of it may seem like nonsense now.
But the next time you flick through, something may
inspire you.*

❻ Real facts

Sometimes research is called for. This might sound an odd thing to do for a fantasy story, but factual accounts of past events can be more extraordinary than fantasy.

- If you want convincing sounding spells, find a book on the history of sorcery and see what new ideas it conjures.

- If you want to create a wonderful castle (below), research different kinds – English, French, Indian, Chinese – then mix them together with some thoughts of your own. You will have something truly original.

❼ Use what you know

You can use your own technical knowledge too. If you play a musical instrument, or know a lot about computers, play chess or practise an unusual sport – archery say, or a martial art – then try blending your own special knowledge with some fantasy characters and see where it takes you. You could suddenly find yourself with a very unusual story to tell.

TIPS AND TECHNIQUES

Ideas can come from anywhere at anytime. J. K. Rowling had nothing to write on when the idea for Harry Potter came to her. She was stuck on a train and that's how the Hogwarts Express was born. Always have your notebook handy.

❽ Use your subconscious mind

Good stories can take time to emerge. Instead of forcing them, try setting your brain the task before you go to sleep. Ask your subconscious mind to come up with some ideas. The next day you may find that your fuzzy thinking has come into sharp focus.

Case study

Robert Louis Stevenson said that the idea for his story, The Strange Case of Dr. Jekyll and Mr Hyde (right) came to him in a dream. Like other well-known writers, he kept a dream diary. Keep a notebook by your bed and write down any good ideas as soon as you wake up – before they burst like bubbles.

❾ Add detail

Once your story ideas start to simmer, help things along by thinking in more detail of the place where the story will take place. Try the exercise in the Now It's Your Turn box again on page 11. Can you feel your ideas developing? Do you need some more…?

❿ Discovering a setting

In fantasy books, the setting is as important as the characters. Think of Narnia or Middle Earth. Now imagine your story's setting. What does the countryside look like? What kind of beings inhabit it? Is it a wild, untamed land or built up with spiring cities? Does your world have different rules from the real world? How will they affect your plot?

⓫ Exciting journeys

You need to know how the places in your world will guide your plot. If your hero needs to go to a special place to complete the quest, then tell the readers something about the place as soon as possible. Use it to build suspense by hinting at the terrible dangers along the way. The more scary or fantastic you make your geography, the more exciting your story can be.

Case study

Paul Stewart, who wrote the Edge Chronicles says the ideas for the books began with illustrator Chris Riddell's map of the place. After that, the books developed as a joint effort – Chris drawing ideas and Paul writing. See the detailed plans in Beyond the Deepwoods *or* The Curse of the Gloamglozer.

TIPS AND TECHNIQUES

In a good fantasy story, your characters' world will always be under some major threat. Read other authors books and see if you can come up with a threat that might pose your hero and their friends a major obstacle to success. It may even be one they might not all be able to overcome...

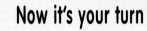

Now it's your turn

Mapping your landscape

In *The Lord of the Rings* (above and left) remember the Mines of Moria, or the Dead Marshes, or the giant spider, Shelob, in her highland lair! In five minutes jot down as many spine-chilling places and monsters that you would like your hero to take on. Now repeat the exercise, listing places with entrancing qualities, e.g. a crystal spring whose waters bestow powers of prophecy. Creating safe havens for your heroes allows them and your readers to draw breath too – or be lulled into a false sense of security! Also when safe havens come under threat by dark forces, readers really care what happens to them.

⑫ Picking details

Once you know your fantasy world really well, pick out only the most striking things to describe. Think brief. Think sharp. Think exciting. From the start, give them vivid clues to trigger their senses. Have something happening at the same time – something mysterious that snags the reader's curiosity.

⑬ Good setting recipe 1

Combine description with action:

> *Among the trees something was happening that was not meant for human eyes…a shaft of blue light cut the darkness. It came from a narrow opening in a high tooth-shaped rock, and within the opening was a pair of iron gates thrown wide, and beyond them a tunnel. Shadows moved on the trees as a strange procession entered through the gates and down into the hill. They were a small people.*
>
> Alan Garner, *The Moon of Gomrath*

⑭ Good setting recipe 2

Combine description with action from a character's point of view:

> *Holly rolled off her futon and stumbled into the shower. That was one advantage of living near the earth's core – the water was always hot. No natural light, of course, but that was a small price to pay for privacy. Underground. The last human-free zone. There was nothing like coming home from a long day on the job, switching off your shield and sinking into a bubbling slime pool. Bliss.*
>
> Eoin Colfer (left), *Artemis Fowl*

Now it's your turn

A striking opening

Write the opening paragraph to your story, and see how you can mix setting descriptions with action. Choose words that fizz – instead of your character walking make him flee, fly or speed through the Grim Gorge. Think of striking images, like Alan Garner's tooth-shaped rock which creates a very sinister atmosphere. Think of using telling adjectives too. Sparkling is stronger than shiny – sparkling does; shiny just is.

⑮ Good setting recipe 3

Combine description with action from a character's point of view and make them in a hurry:

> *Holly grabbed the remains of a nettle smoothie from the cooler and drank it in the tunnels. As usual there was chaos in the main thoroughfare. Airborne sprites jammed the avenue like stones in a bottle. The gnomes weren't helping either, lumbering along with their big swinging behinds blocking two lanes. Swear toads infested every damp patch, cursing like sailors.*
>
> Eoin Colfer, *Artemis Fowl*

⑯ Good setting recipe 4

If your fantasy world needs a lot of explanation, set the scene in the first chapter and you won't have to use so much description later on. This device is employed by C.S. Lewis:

> *This must be a simply enormous wardrobe! thought Lucy... Then she noticed that there was something crunching under her feet... But instead of feeling the hard, smooth wood of the floor of the wardrobe she felt something soft and powdery and extremely cold... Lucy felt a little frightened but she felt very inquisitive and excited too.*
>
> C.S. Lewis, *The Lion, The Witch and the Wardrobe*

HEROES

The key to successful stories is devising believable heroes, villains and a valuable supporting cast. The main thing when creating a hero, such as King Arthur (right), is that you must care deeply about them, otherwise you won't be able to make the readers care about them.

❶ Finding a hero's name

Philip Pullman says Lyra from *Northern Lights* stepped into his mind fully formed, name and all. J. K. Rowling collects words she likes the sound of. Dumbledore means bumblebee in Old English. If you're stuck, flick through a baby names book, an atlas index or telephone book. If you make a name up, say it out loud to see what it sounds like.

TIPS AND TECHNIQUES

Start a 'special words' list in your notebook. Write down any word that catches your imagination. You'll know where to look the next time you are stuck for a name. Don't make it too complicated for readers to remember. Simple names like Kit, Gem or Will can often be more memorable.

❷ Build up a picture

You need to know what your hero looks like. Think about their clothes, their hair, height and build, what they like and don't like. Are they good at something? What are their weaknesses? Think how their weaknesses might play a part in your story. For instance, Lyra is a liar. She also lacks imagination, but both of these flaws often help her out of tough situations.

Now it's your turn

Know your hero

Your hero needs a past. Brainstorm everything you can think of in five minutes – who they are, where they live, whether they have a family, go to work or school. Here is Eoin Colfer's brief history of Holly Short (right) in *Artemis Fowl*:

Technically she was an elf, fairy being a general term. She was a leprechaun too, but that was just a job…Cupid was her great-grandfather. Her mother was a European elf with a fiery temper and a willowy frame.

❸ What's the problem?

Finally, and most importantly, YOUR HERO NEEDS A PROBLEM! Or several. No one wants to read stories about people with perfect, happy lives. In the *Harry Potter* series, Harry's life is blighted by his cruel adoptive family, the Dursleys (right). Use your own experiences to make your hero's problems real.

Your readers will only keep reading if they feel for your characters. You must describe some real emotions. Tap into your own.

❹ What kind of baddy?

As your hero must have problems to deal with, your villain will provide the external problem or conflict. So who is your villain? Does the one you dealt yourself in the brainstorming exercise on page 17 look promising?

❺ Motivation for evil

First think about what makes your villains so evil. Are they hungry for power? Do they want great wealth or some special knowledge that will help them control everyone, or make them immortal? Are they simply cruel and get their pleasure from destroying things, such as Count Olaf (left) in *A Series of Unfortunate Events*? Are they envious of your hero – a rival for some title or position? Reared by uncaring guardians? Or has it simply never occurred to them to be good?

Now it's your turn

Know your villain

In a ten-minute practice, brainstorm your villain. How does he operate and what is his motivation? Think about his weaknesses too and how these might help the story. For example, in the *Harry Potter* books, Voldemort can only understand love of power and not love itself.

IDEAS FILE

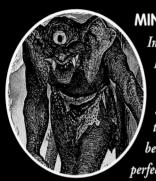

MINDLESS EVIL

In *The BFG*, Roald Dahl has nine man-eating giants who think their grim behaviour is perfectly fine.

LURKING EVIL

Then there are other evil beings that we hardly see, like Philip Ridley's giant crocodile, Krindlekrax, who inhabits the sewers of Lizard Street. Or Terry Pratchett's rat king, Spider, who tries to melt Maurice's brain in *The Amazing Maurice and his Educated Rodents*.

SUBTLE VILLAINS

Finally there are villains who are hard to spot because they are so charming, such as Lyra's glamourous mother, Mrs Coulter. She hardly ever gives herself away. Instead, her true nature is revealed to us by the malicious behaviour of her golden monkey daemon.

WORLD DOMINATION

Sauron (below) in *The Lord of the Rings* is one of the most frightening villains ever. He is too evil to be wholly described. His evil corrupts many others: the terrifying Black Riders and Orcs; the once good Saruman; the miserable Gollum; and it causes the grim desolation of Mordor.

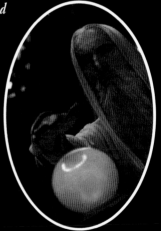

TIPS AND TECHNIQUES

The more you question your villains, the more you'll find out about them, and the more intriguing they'll become. The most frightening thing of all is something that you can't quite see! The more complex your villain, the bigger the battle for your hero, and the more exciting your story.

❻ The rest of the cast

In fantasy, as in real life, your heroes will be judged by the company they keep. Scenes between hero and friends are a good way to show the reader what he or she is really like as a person. How would we know how loyal Harry Potter is without seeing him with his friends (left).

❼ Goodies vs Baddies

You will need 'goodies' and 'baddies' to help or harm your hero. In the brainstorming exercise on page 17, you dealt yourself a hero's helper and a villain's henchman. Can you now develop these ideas? Make up your own beings, or adapt some from a host of marvellous fantasy creatures in myths and fairy tales. What about a villain such as Gollum (right) in the *Lord of the Rings* trilogy, or a winged horse like Pegasus who might whisk your hero to safety, or some variation on the snake-headed Medusa from Greek myth, who could turn a person to stone just by looking at them?

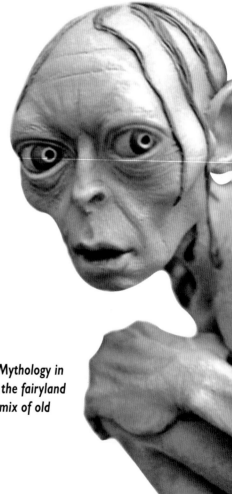

TIPS AND TECHNIQUES

For extraordinary creatures find a Dictionary of World Mythology in the library. See what you can recycle. In Artemis Fowl the fairyland security expert is a centaur – half-man, half-horse. The mix of old with new can make a wonderfully original character.

Now it's your turn

CETUS
ARGUS
SPHINX
MEDUSA

Picture your characters

In your next practice, try sketching your characters. Ask your creations what special powers they have and how these will make your story more exciting. Hunt for good names that tell the reader something about the character. Remember that your characters each need some special quality or flaw that will make them instantly more marvellous or dastardly.

❽ The mark of a character

In *The Lord of the Rings*, Frodo seems an unlikely hero to take on the impossible quest against the mighty Sauron. One way that Tolkien makes us think that he has hidden qualities is by showing us his friend Sam's unshakeable devotion to him.

❾ Creature concoction

A creature from Greek mythology has the hind parts of a dragon, the body of a goat, the forelegs of a lion and the head of each. Mixed in equal proportions, and abracadabra! – you have a Chimera (above). Can you come up with any scary creature combinations? *Tyrannosaurus Rex* meets Giant Vampire Bat meets…?

WHO'S SPEAKING?

Before you write your opening line, you need to decide if you want to tell the story from one particular person's point of view – say your hero. Or do you want your readers to know everything that is happening to all your characters at once? You decide...

❶ An all-seeing view

Most fantasy stories and fairy tales are written using the omniscient or 'all-seeing' view. This means you can tell readers how the hero feels when he is locked up in the dungeon, what his jailer thinks, and then describe the blast of dragon's breath that is burning down the East Tower, which neither the hero nor the jailer can see, but you the author can. In *A Series of Unfortunate Events* (right), Lemony Snicket uses the all-seeing view in a way that adds to the dark humour of the stories. C. S. Lewis and Roald Dahl also show us what their different characters are feeling and thinking.

It was an unpleasant evening. Lucy was miserable and Edmund was beginning to feel his plan wasn't working as well as expected. The two older children were beginning to think that Lucy was out of her mind. They stood in the passage talking...in whispers long after she had gone to bed.

C. S. Lewis, *The Lion, the Witch and the Wardrobe*

❷ The third person

Another way is to pick your hero's point of view and tell the story from how she or he sees everything, usually written in the third person past tense. You can write it from the viewpoints of different characters too, set down in alternating chapters and this can add suspense. In Cynthia Voigt's *The Wings of a Falcon*, the story opens from the point of view of a nameless boy. Instantly we are right inside his head, sharing his fears:

> *He knew from the first that this man would know how to hurt him. He had to keep the fear secret, and he couldn't cry no matter how much he wanted to.*
>
> Cynthia Voigt, *The Wings of a Falcon*

❸ The first person

The first person point of view can be an exciting way of telling a story. When you say 'I did this' or 'I saw that', it's much easier to persuade the reader that everything you say is true. But it is no longer possible to know what the other characters are thinking, except when they are talking:

> *Tumber Hill! It's my clamber-and-tumble-and-beech-and-bramble hill! Sometimes, when I'm standing on the top, I fill my lungs with air and I shout. I shout!*
>
> Kevin Crossley-Holland, *Arthur:The Seeing Stone*

Now it's your turn

Find your point of view

Write a scene from your own story. Describe your hero battling with some villain. First write it as the omniscient, all-knowing narrator, then re-write it in the third person, from your hero's and villain's viewpoint. Finally, try it in the first person. Read your efforts aloud to yourself. Which one do you prefer and why?

READY TO WRITE

When your story starts bubbling fiercely in your mind, it's a good idea to write a few paragraphs about it. Tell the story of your story. This is your synopsis and will help you keep your story on track. Reveal just enough to be intriguing but don't give away the end.

❶ Back cover inspiration

To get some ideas, look at the back covers of some fantasy books and read the blurb. See how it says just enough about the hero, villain and all the problems to make the reader want to read more. It conveys tone too, indicating whether the book is serious or humourous. The blurb from *The Bad Beginning* by Lemony Snicket (right) conjures up a menacing air:

> *Dear Reader,*
> *I'm sorry to say that the book you are holding in your hands is extremely unpleasant. It tells an unhappy tale about three very unlucky children. From the very first page of the book, disaster lurks at their heels. One might say they are magnets for misfortune.*
>
> Lemony Snicket, *The Bad Beginning*

Now it's your turn

Write your blurb

Sum up your story in a single striking sentence, then develop it in two or three short paragraphs. Think about your potential readers and try to draw them in to make them want to read the book.

❷ Create a synopsis

Before they start writing, novelists often list all their chapters, saying briefly what will happen in each chapter episode. This is called a chapter synopsis, and it provides a writer with a skeleton plot, which like the general synopsis, helps keep them on track as they write. To help them, they map out the plot (the sequence of events) in a series of sketches called storyboards. You can do this for your story. Draw the main episodes in pictures. Add a few notes that say what is happening in each scene.

❸ Make a Story Map

Now you have a synopsis that says what your story is about; a cast of characters; a setting; and you know from whose viewpoint you wish to tell the tale. A useful tool is a story map. Before film-makers can start filming, they must know the main story episodes and decide how they can best tell their story in filmed images.

TIPS AND TECHNIQUES

If you can't sum up your story as simply as these extracts, it is possibly too complicated. Simplify it. As you work on your own synopsis, start asking yourself 'Whose story is this and how will I tell it?'

❹ Get inspiration from a classic

Here are some storyboard captions for the novel *Peter Pan* (right) by J.M. Barrie.

1. Peter Pan sneaks in to listen to the Darling children's bedtime stories;
2. Peter teaches Wendy, John and Michael to fly and takes them to Neverland;
3. Egged on by a jealous Tinkerbell, the Lost Boys, shoot at Wendy;
4. Peter banishes Tinkerbell for a week and tells the Lost Boys he has brought Wendy to look after them;
5. Captain Hook (below) wants revenge on Peter, who cut off his arm and threw it to the crocodile.
6. Peter rescues Tiger Lily at Marooners' Rock; she and her tribe become his ally;
7. Wendy wants to go home and take the Lost Boys
8. Pirates capture Wendy and the boys;
9. Peter saves them all and Hook eaten by the crocodile;
10. The children take the Lost Boys home, but Peter Pan stays in Neverland.

❺ Decide to write a novel?

Novels aren't short stories made longer, but short stories made fatter. They still have beginnings, middles and ends, but the main story is expanded with subplots and many more characters and incidents. If you choose to write a novel, then a chapter synopsis will help you map out the

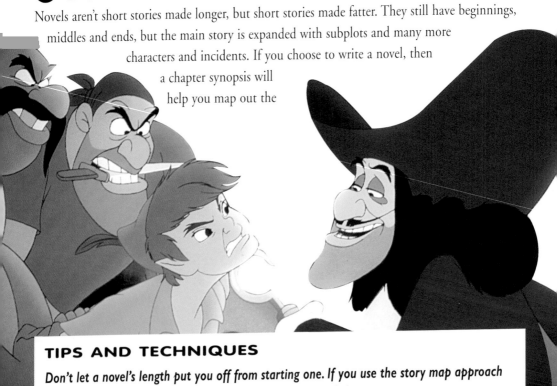

TIPS AND TECHNIQUES

Don't let a novel's length put you off from starting one. If you use the story map approach it is often easier to write a novel than it is to write a good short story.

plot and decide which characters you will need to develop the story. Each chapter heading is then spun out, like a mini-story inside the larger story. Dividing the story into chapters also helps build suspense. If you end a chapter on a cliffhanger, and then switch to another character's story in the next chapter, you will have your readers hooked.

❻ Or a short story...

If you want to write a short story, then mapping out the key scenes like the *Peter Pan* (left and right) example will also help you pace your story, and focus on the most exciting events and characters. It may also throw up any flaws in your plot, so you can fix them before you start writing. For example, a short story version of Peter Pan would probably need to cut out some of the scenes listed above, and develop Peter Pan's character in more detail.

Now it's your turn

Weave a story web

If you are struggling with your story map, try this exercise.

In the middle of a large piece of paper, draw a rough sketch of your hero within a circle. As you are drawing, imagine that you are that hero, trying to decide which way to go. Think about the problems they have and what they are going to do about them? Draw six spokes around your hero circle. Each leads to another circle. Inside each one sketch a different scene, or write it as notes. Each circle will be some new course of action that you might take, or some obstacle that an enemy sets in your path. Give yourself 20 minutes. You may be surprised how your story starts growing.

❼ Heroic beginnings

Once you have your idea ready, have split your story into scenes and planned your plot properly you are ready to start telling your own story. Focus on your hero. How will you win the readers to their cause?

❽ Find your hook

The first part of your story will often introduce the main characters, shows your readers the problems and conflicts and starts the heroes off on their quest to resolve all their difficulties. As you write the opening scenes, imagine you are trying to convince your friends to join you on a hazardous journey. Pull out all the stops!

❾ Starting points

But where to start your story exactly? What is the opening scene? In *The Wizard of Oz* the external conflict is very dramatic. No sooner have we learned all about the greyness of Dorothy's Kansas life (left), than the cyclone hits and blows her and Toto away. But by showing a little of 'what went before', the back story, the

writer creates more drama when the conflict actually comes. In *The Bad Beginning* (above), narrator Lemony Snicket starts by setting readers a challenge they can't resist, as well as making them wonder: what story could possibly be so awful?

If you are interested in stories with happy endings, you would be better off reading some other book. In this book, not only is there no happy ending, there is no happy beginning and very few happy things in the middle.

Lemony Snicket, *The Bad Beginning*

TIPS AND TECHNIQUES

Hooking your readers should start from your story's first sentence and paragraph. Study as many story openings as you can find. Which ones work best and why? Make your opening mysterious, or dramatic, or funny. Write it and re-write it. Read it aloud. Introduce the conflict straight away or soon afterwards. Send your heroes on their way...

⓾ False happy endings

If beginnings must grip, then 'middles' should grip harder. Find ways to add more complications. Start fattening your story by increasing the conflicts. One way to create tension and drama is to have a false happy ending. This is when the hero thinks they have solved their problems or defeated the villain, and everyone breathes a sigh of relief. This makes it double scary when the enemy rears their ugly head once more. Also readers start wondering, will the hero fail to defeat them next time too?

⓫ Creating character conflict

Misunderstandings between the characters can add drama and thicken the plot. Perhaps a supporting character has started something that the hero doesn't know about – some kind act that goes wrong, or a deliberate act of betrayal. In *The Lion, the Witch and the Wardrobe*, by C. S. Lewis, Edmund's sub-plot adds suspense to the main story, driving it on at a more exciting pace. It also adds complications to the sibling relationships and makes the reader wonder how they will be resolved.

In *The Lion, the Witch and the Wardrobe* (right), the early part of the story is about Lucy trying to make Susan and Peter believe that she has been to another world called Narnia. Next comes the second story-line of Edmund's meeting with the White Witch. His denials make things worse for Lucy. But when all four children step through the wardrobe, Edmund's nasty game is exposed and seemingly resolved until… he sneaks off to betray all.

⑫ Explore weaknesses

Using your hero's weaknesses can add more twists and suspense to the story. In *Artemis Fowl*, Holly Short has been so busy with her career that for four years she has put off performing the ritual to renew her fairy power. Anxious not to lose face, she lies to her boss about this, and so is running low on power when she is sent on a dangerous mission to track an escaped troll. The mission almost goes wrong… giving Artemis Fowl the chance he needs to snatch a leprechaun with her defences down.

TIPS AND TECHNIQUES

Action scenes should spring from the characters' own plans, not from your need to revive a flagging story.
But when you do include them, make them as exciting as possible.

⑬ Maintain the action

Keep your characters busy at all times, on the move, working things out, coming to the wrong conclusions, having fights, escaping disasters.

Think of Harry, Hermione and Ron (top) trying to save the Philosopher's Stone:

> *They seized a broomstick each and kicked off into the air, soaring into the midst of the cloud of keys. They grabbed and snatched but the bewitched keys darted and dived …*
>
> J. K. Rowling, *Harry Potter and the Philosopher's Stone*

⑭ Dramatic climaxes

In the last part of your story, the hero's problems must reach a dramatic climax. After this, the problems will be resolved. The story will end, usually with a reference to the story's beginning. Your hero may go back to the old life that readers saw at the story's start, but something important will have changed.

⑮ Happy endings

Most readers like a happy ending of some sort, and this is perhaps the hardest part of story writing. You must satisfy your readers' need for this, while avoiding being predictable.

⑯ Painful lessons

Your heroes will have gained and learned something, but they might have lost something, too. In *The Lord of the Rings*, the climax of Frodo's story occurs at Mount Doom where the ring is finally destroyed. How it happens is an unexpected twist, but the quest is a success and the evil Sauron has been defeated. But Frodo has paid a high price for this victory – he can't go back to his old cosy life in the Shire. It is Sam who goes back to rescue the Shire, taking the story back to where it started; the same place but no longer the same.

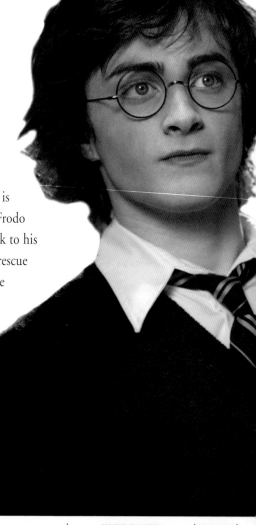

Now its your turn

Choose your own ending

Read the ending of your favourite fantasy book then think about what you liked about it, and what you didn't. Would you have ended the story differently and if so, how? If you do change it, come back to your version after a break and re-read it. Do you still think you are right?

⑰ New beginnings

Up-beat endings that suggest more story, make readers happy. In *Harry Potter and the Philosopher's Stone* (left) the climax comes with Harry's defeat of Voldemort. But then Rowling returns us to where the story started: face to face with the dreadful Dursleys. But before it turns into an anti-climax, she lets readers know that Harry is indeed older and wiser. When Hermione wishes him a good holiday, he shocks her by saying *'They don't know that we're not allowed to use magic at home. I'm going to have a lot of fun with Dudley this summer.'* The readers grin at the thought of Harry getting his own back!

Bad endings are ones that:

• Fizzle out because you've run out of ideas;

• Rely on some coincidence or surprise magic that hasn't been mentioned in the story;

• Fail to show how the characters have changed in some way;

• Are too grim and depressing and leave the reader with no hope.

TIPS AND TECHNIQUES

Good stories may seem to go in straight lines: beginning, middle, end, but they also go round in circles. The ending should always have some link with the beginning.

MAKING WORDS WORK

Words are precious, and like magic wishes, are best used sparingly. When you write, make each word work hard for your story. Use the most vivid or powerful words you can think of.

❶ Use similes

In *Arthur: The Seeing Stone*, Kevin Crossley-Holland uses many unusual **similes**. The beech trees sound 'like whispering spirits'; Merlin (left) has 'slateshine eyes' while Lady Alice's are 'the colour of ripe hazelnuts'. He uses **metaphors** too. Ygerna is 'so frozen with grief she cannot even melt into tears'. And we know that she is feeling truly terrible.

❷ Change the rhythm and length of your sentences

If something frightening is going to happen, pace the writing to build suspense. Spin out the phrases as you write using choice pieces of description; imagine yourself creeping up on your reader – then strike!

TIPS AND TECHNIQUES

Action scenes should stick to the action and should not be too drawn out. Use short, punchy phrases and limit description to the bare minimum. Try ending a dramatic scene on a cliffhanger. Leave your heroes in peril and drive your readers to find out what happens next.

❸ Use dramatic irony

Dramatic irony is another useful device. This is where the reader knows something important that the characters don't know . In *A Series of Unfortunate Events* (right), Lemony Snicket uses dramatic irony in all his stories – forewarning us of the horrible things that are going to happen, just when the characters are having a moment's happiness.

④ Change the mood

Changes in mood can increase or decrease drama, as well as give readers some variety. Tolkien has written much of *The Lord of the Rings* in a doom-laden tone, but if it were like this from start to finish, the 'doominess' would lose its power and the readers' interest. To avoid this, Tolkien weaves in many happier, light-hearted episodes, full of enchantment, which give readers a rest from the high tension. Also, when evil rears its head again, it seems so much worse after the pleasant interlude.

⑤ Crank up suspense and drama

Foreshadowing is an essential tool in all fiction writing. It means dropping hints about coming events. In the *Harry Potter* books, remarks about the fate of Harry's family are used to remind us of Voldemort, sometimes with just a hint of worry, sometimes to stir up some real fear. And whenever Harry's scar starts throbbing (above), we know Voldemort is on the prowl.

> *It was a unicorn all right, and it was dead … Harry had taken one step towards it when a slithering sound made him freeze where he stood. A bush on the edge of the clearing quivered…Then out of the shadows, a hooded figure came crawling like some stalking beast…*
>
> J. K. Rowling, *Harry Potter and the Philosopher's Stone*

CREATING DIALOGUE

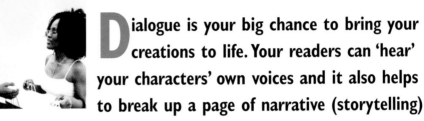

Dialogue is your big chance to bring your creations to life. Your readers can 'hear' your characters' own voices and it also helps to break up a page of narrative (storytelling) giving readers' eyes a rest. It is a powerful storytelling tool – one that can add colour, pace, mood and suspense to your story.

❶ Let your characters speak for themselves

The best way to learn about dialogue is to switch on your listening ear and eavesdrop. Tune into the way people phrase their words. Write down any good idioms – someone saying 'sling yer hook' or 'shove off' instead of 'go away'. Watch people's body language too when they are whispering or arguing. Look, listen and absorb...

TIPS AND TECHNIQUES

When writing dialogue, don't just stick to 'he said/she said' all the time. Use words like 'asked', 'replied', 'exclaimed', 'cried', 'whispered', etc. to create excitement and variety in your writing.

❷ Following convention

The way dialogue is written down follows conventions or rules too. It is usual to start a new paragraph with every new speaker. What they say is enclosed in single or double inverted commas, followed by 'he said' or 'she said' to indicate the speaker. Other information may be added, such as the speaker's feelings or actions. See too, how inserting tags in the middle of some speech lines, gives the impression of a real conversation – reading aloud, this actually creates a rhythmic flow that makes the exchanges easier to follow.

Case study

As a child, Kate DiCamillo suffered from chronic pneumonia, and entertained herself by reading. When she was in her twenties, she discovered a new love for children's books, and began writing her own. Perhaps because of her background, dialogue is very important in her books. She describes **Because of Winn-Dixie** as "a hymn to dogs, friendship, and the South."

"Would it be possible for me to have a last word with the princess?" Despereaux asked. "A word?" said the second hood. "You want a word with a human?" "I want to tell her what happened to me." "Geez," said the first hood. He stopped and stamped a paw on the floor in frustration. "Cripes. You can't learn can you."

Kate DiCamillo (right), *The Tale of Despereaux*

Now it's your turn

Writing a good argument

Remember an argument you had or heard. Fictionalise it, change the names but pour anger into the words. Don't rely on tags like 'yelled' or 'screamed' to show the mood. Think too: the speakers are trying to hurt each other! Their words will fire off like bullets or build quietly to a fatal blow depending on their character. When you have finished, read it aloud. Now revise it. Take out any unnecessary 'saids'. Cut down all the spoken words to the bare bones, then read it aloud once more. You are learning another absolutely essential writing skill – the art of editing your own work.

❸ Fictional eavesdropping

Details about a place or your character's history and motivation can be told much more swiftly in a conversation between two characters. It is more interesting – as any eavesdropping always is, even the fictional sort. In J. M. Barrie's *Peter Pan*, the conversation between Smee and Captain Hook (below) briefly explain Hook's hatred for Peter Pan:

> *"I have often," said Smee, "noticed your strange dread of crocodiles." "Not of crocodiles," Hook corrected him, "but of that one crocodile. It liked my arm so much, Smee, that it has followed me ever since, from sea to sea and from land to land, licking its lips for the rest of me." "In a way," said Smee, "it's a sort of compliment." "I want no such compliments," Hook barked petulantly. "I want Peter Pan, who first gave the brute its taste for me."*
>
> J. M. Barrie, *Peter Pan*

❹ Creating atmosphere

Dialogue can be used to create different atmospheres. In *The Curse of the Gloamglozer*, the words of Linius Pallitax, the Most High Academe, create both immediate suspense and a sense of bad things to come:

> *"And close the door," Linius added. His voice dropped to an urgent whisper. "I don't want a single word of what I'm about to say to go beyond these four walls. Is that understood?"*
>
> Paul Stewart and Chris Riddell, *The Curse of the Gloamglozer*

⑤ Give direct opinions

If you are writing from a limited viewpoint (third or first person), then using dialogue is the only way that readers can hear other characters' opinions directly. Terry Pratchett does this brilliantly in *The Johnny Maxwell Trilogy* where the stories are told from Johnny's viewpoint. He uses dialogue to express the characters' views of each other. In the following extract, Johnny takes Wobbler, Bigmac and Yo-less to the cemetery to prove he can see dead people:

> *"I don't know as this is right," said Wobbler, when the four of them had gathered by the gate.*
> *"There's crosses all over the place," said Yo-less.*
> *"Yes, but I'm an atheist," said Wobbler.*
> *"Then you shouldn't believe in ghosts –"*
> *"Post-living citizens," Bigmac corrected him.*
> *"Bigmac?" said Johnny.*
> *"Yeah?"*
> *"What're you holding behind your back?" Wobbler craned to see.*
> *"It's bit of sharpened wood," he reported. "And a hammer."*
> *"Bigmac!"*
>
> Terry Pratchett, *Johnny and the Dead*

TIPS AND TECHNIQUES

As you write your own stories, be on the look out for description or explanatory passages that would be better as dialogue. Dialogue is never idle chit chat. It moves the story on, by revealing the characters and their circumstances, and by speeding up the telling.

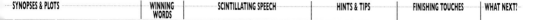

❻ Find different ways of speaking

When writing fantasy, it is tempting to devise some other-worldly way for your characters to speak. This is hard to keep up, and may sound false to the reader. A better way is to simply suggest a different way of speaking.

❼ Poetic speech

In *The Wizard of Earthsea*, Ursula K. Le Guin uses stately language, reminiscent of much older forms of English, but still easy to understand.

> *Then he summoned the dragon: "Usurper of Pendor, come defend your hoard!" and "Eight sons I had, little wizard," said the great dry voice of the dragon.*
>
> Ursula K. Le Guin, *The Wizard of Earthsea*

❽ Invent language

Of course there will always be writers whose sheer inventiveness does let them do the inadvisable. In *The BFG* Roald Dahl invents a whole new vocabulary for his friendly giant. But because the creations remind us, by sound or suggestion, of proper words, we know what he means.

> *"Redunculous!" said the BFG. "If everyone is making whizzpoppers, then why not talk about it? We is now having a swiggle of this delicious frobscottle and you will see the happy result."*
>
> Roald Dahl, *The BFG*

❾ Use accents

In the *Harry Potter* books, Hagrid has a Scottish accent but J. K. Rowling only suggests it in some dialogue and in the rhythm of his speech.

> *Just Ollivanders left now – only place fer wands, Ollivanders, and yeh gotta have the best wand.*
>
> J. K. Rowling, *Harry Potter and the Philosopher's Stone*

❿ Social class

Dialogue should also reveal differences in education or social class. In *The Tale of Despereaux* the Princess Pea sounds very different from the uneducated Miggery Sow.

> *"Soup! Gor! That's against the law." "Yes," said the princess, "my father outlawed it because my mother died while she was eating it." "Your ma's dead?" "Yes," said the Pea. "She died just last month." She bit her bottom lip to stop it from trembling. "Ain't that the thing?" said Mig. "My ma is dead too."*
>
> Kate DiCamillo, *The Tale of Despereaux*

⑪ Age differences

In *Artemis Fowl*, Eoin Colfer reverses the usual adult-talking-down-to-child pattern as young Artemis often speaks to the adult Butler as if he were the child. The following three lines give a snapshot of their unusual relationship:

"I hope this isn't another wild-goose chase, Butler," Artemis said, his voice soft and clipped. "Especially after Cairo." "No, sir. I'm certain this time. Nguyen is a good man." "Hmm," droned Artemis, unconvinced.

Eoin Colfer, *Artemis Fowl*

Now it's your turn

Pirate talk

Imagine you are eavesdropping on Captain Hook and Smee. They are discussing a host of different ways to kill Peter Pan and the Lost Boys. First make a list of a few nasty ideas they might come up with. Then think about Captain Hook and Smee as characters. They are both villains, but one is cruel and ferocious and the other more sly. Now write down their conversation, and see if you can give each character their own voice. Invent your own mannerisms if you want to. When you have finished, edit the piece, cutting out all unnecessary words. Then read it aloud and see if it flows. Make more improvements. Read it aloud again. Dialogue always takes a lot of re-writing.

BEATING WRITING PROBLEMS

Sometimes even the keenest writers can find they have no words. This is called writer's block and it can last for hours or years. But what are the causes and how can they be overcome?

❶ Get over your insecurities

Do you remember the Story Spectre, first mentioned on page 11. This is your internal critic who tells you what you have written is no good and eventually drives you back to the TV or gameboy. If this happens, brainstorm some lists or write about your favourite things or the best thing that has ever happened to you.

❷ Find fresh ideas

Another form of block is thinking that you have nothing to say. Again, if you are writing and exercising regularly, you know that you can trigger ideas at the

Now it's your turn

Positive thinking

Write on the cover of your notebook: *Writing is magic, but it is not always easy!*

Now brainstorm for five minutes, listing all the things you find difficult about writing. Repeat the exercise, only this time list all the things you love about writing. Now look over the problems. Are these things that can be fixed with more time and practice and a lot more reading? Is learning to write more important to you than the problems? If the answer is 'yes', then give yourself five gold stars. You are still on the quest. Your stories will get written.

drop of a hat. You are also training yourself to write when you don't exactly feel like it. If all writers waited for inspiration to strike, nothing much would be written.

❸ Responding to criticism

No one enjoys rejection or criticism, but it is an important part of learning to be a writer. If you invite someone to read your stories, you have to prepare yourself for negative comments. As you develop your writing skills, you will develop faith in yourself. You will see rejection as a chance to re-write your story, if it really needs it.

❹ Don't assume other writers are better than you

This is a common trap into which even experienced writers fall. How good a writer you become is up to you and how hard you want to work at it.

Only you can tell your stories, and every new one is an addition to the great human story treasure-house. Read other writers' work to help you improve. Be grateful for their guidance, but don't envy them.

Case study

J. R. Tolkien said he was stuck in the Mines of Moria (below) for a whole year because he couldn't work out what would happen next to his characters. But the long wait was clearly worth it.

❺ Understanding writer's block

The kind of writer's block that leaves you stuck mid-story, usually means there has not been enough planning. Maybe some horrible flaw in your plot has cropped up and looks like ruining everything. Don't panic! There will be an answer.

❻ Interrogate your characters

One way to sort out a story block is to play the 'What If' game, as you did on page 15. Interrogate your key characters in the same way. Build up a web of questions to start building possible new story strands. Some of these could well take the story forward in a new way and add some interesting complications.

❼ Role play

Writing is a lonely activity, so why not turn your writing problem into a game with friends or family. Give them character roles to play and see what the dialogue between you conjures up.

TIPS AND TECHNIQUES

Give your character no peace until you know exactly what the quest is. If nothing can spark inspiration for you, you could walk the dog, or clean out your bedroom to unwind. Doing tasks that give your mind a rest could be just the thing to spring an idea.

❽ Keep a journal

Write about life at school or home, record all the details of your hobbies and interests. Set yourself a minimum target length for each entry, say 300 words. If you use a computer for writing you can count them easily. Make a note. Never write less than your target, even if it means describing the pattern on your bedroom wallpaper or what's in your sandwich. But try to write more. And look for ways of turning the day's events into an anecdote. Did your best friend have a row with her parents? Write about it. Write how you would feel if you were them.

❾ Group brainstorming

If your key character isn't coming to life, brainstorm with your friends. Start by writing a brief character description on the top of a sheet of paper. When your time is up, pass it to a friend to add their ideas to yours. Don't worry about complete sentences. Thoughts are what count. When two minutes are up, the paper is passed on to the next person. Mull over the results. Have you learned something about your character that you didn't know before?

❿ Be zany!

If you still think you have absolutely nothing to say, try this. Give yourself ten minutes to describe the most boring, mind-numbing thing you can think of. Say how you survived the experience. Or maybe you didn't. Maybe it turned you into some other life form that just pretends to be you. Be funny, melodramatic, or downright ridiculous. Write it to entertain your friends.

PREPARING YOUR WORK

When your story has been 'resting' in your desk for a month, take it out and have a read through it. You will be able to see your work with fresh eyes and spot flaws more easily.

❶ Editing

Reading your work aloud will help you to simplify rambling sentences and correct dialogue that doesn't flow. Cut out all unnecessary adjectives and adverbs and words like 'very'. This will instantly make your writing crisper. Once you have cut down the number of words, decide how well the story works. Does it have a satisfying end? Has your hero resolved the conflict in the best possible way? When your story is as good as can be, write it out afresh, or type it up on a computer. This is your manuscript.

❷ Think of a title

The Amber SPYGLASS

Harry Potter and the HALF BLOOD PRINCE

It is important to think of a really good title – something intriguing and eye catching. Think about some titles you know.

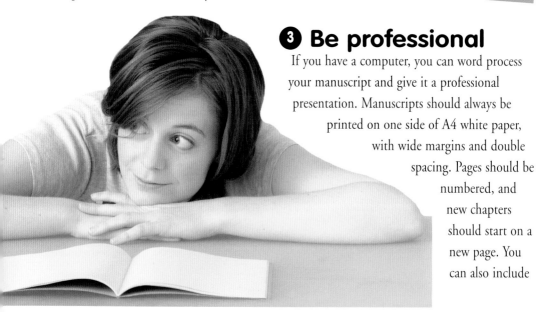

❸ Be professional

If you have a computer, you can word process your manuscript and give it a professional presentation. Manuscripts should always be printed on one side of A4 white paper, with wide margins and double spacing. Pages should be numbered, and new chapters should start on a new page. You can also include

your title as a header on the top of each page. At the front, you should have a title page, with your name, address, telephone number and email address on it. Repeat this information on the last page.

❹ Make your own book

If your school has its own publishing lab, why not use it to 'publish' your own story or make a class story anthology (collection). A computer will let you choose your own font (print style) or justify the text (making even length margins like a professionally printed page). When you have typed and saved your story to a file, you can edit it quickly with the spell- and grammar checker, or move sections of your story around using the 'cut and paste' facility, which saves a lot of rewriting. Having your story on a computer file also means you can print several copies or revise the whole story if you want to.

❺ Design a cover

Once your story is in good shape, you can print it out and then use the computer to design the cover. A graphics program will let you scan and print your own artwork, or download ready-made graphics. Or you could use your own digital photographs and learn how to manipulate them on screen to produce some highly original images. You can use yourself or friends as 'models' for your story's heroes.

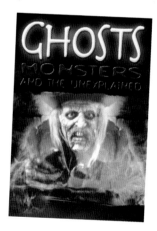

TIPS AND TECHNIQUES

Whether you type up your story on a computer or do it by hand, always make a copy before you give it to anyone else to read in case the manuscript is lost!

❻ Some places to publish your story

The next step is to find an audience for your fantasy fiction. Family members or classmates may be receptive. Or you may want to publish your work via a publishing house or online site. There are magazines and a number of writing websites that accept stories and novel chapters from young writers. Some have chat rooms and some give writing advice too and run regular competitions. Each site has its own rules about submitting work to them, so make sure you read them carefully before you send in a story. See page 62 for more details. You can also:

- Send things to your school magazine, or if your school doesn't have a magazine, then start your own with like-minded friends.

- Keep your eyes peeled when reading your local newspaper or your favourite comics and magazines. They might be running a writing competition that you can submit something to.

- Keep an eye open at local museums and colleges. Some run creative writing workshops during school vacations.

❼ Writing clubs

Starting a writing club or critique group and exchanging stories is a great way of getting your fantasy stories out there. It will also get you used to criticism from others, which will prove invaluable in learning how to write. Your local library might be kind enough to provide a forum for such a club.

❽ Finding a publisher

Secure any submission with a paperclip and always enclose a short letter (saying what you have sent) and a stamped, addressed envelope for the story's return. Study the market and find out which publishing houses are most likely to publish fantasy fiction. Addresses of publishing houses and information about whether they accept submissions can be found in writers' handbooks. Bear in mind that manuscripts that haven't been asked for or paid for by a publisher – unsolicited submissions – are rarely published.

❾ Some famous rejections

Even though Allen & Unwin had successfully published Tolkien's *The Hobbit* in 1936, they rejected *The Lord of the Rings* at first, thinking adults wouldn't read a hobbit book. It had taken Tolkien over ten years to write. L. Frank Baum had his *The Wizard of Oz* story rejected by the Hill Company because the publishers didn't like the original title, *The Emerald City*. They thought it unlucky!

If the difficulties of having your work published make you downhearted, have faith! If you really want to be a published writer, you will find a way.

❿ Writer's tip

If your story is rejected by an editor, see it as a chance to make it better. Try again! But remember…having your work published is wonderful, but it is not the only thing! Being able to make up a story is a gift, so why not give yours to someone you love? Read it to a younger brother or sister. Tell it to your grandmother.
Find your audience!

TIPS AND TECHNIQUES

*READ, READ, READ,
WRITE, WRITE, WRITE.*

It's the only writing spell you will ever need.

Case study

Philip Pullman began his storytelling career as a child. He loved comics and used to make up his own stories to tell his younger brother and friends. After a time he began to write his own stories down.

WHEN YOU'VE FINISHED YOUR STORY

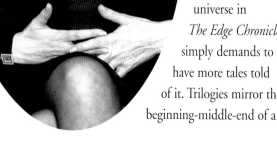

Completing your first story is a wonderful achievement. You have started to master your writer's craft and probably learned a lot about yourself too. But now, you must seek out another quest. You have several options.

❶ How about a sequel?

When thinking about your next work, ask yourself: 'Can I write a sequel and develop the story? Each *Harry Potter* book for example, is a complete story, but the characters and the conflicts with Voldemort continue and develop from book to book.

J. K. Rowling (left) gives a summary of Harry's back story near the start of her books, so that if someone reads one out of order, they can still understand and enjoy the story. She planned to have a seven-book series right from the start: a book for each year of Harry's training at Hogwarts.

❷ Trilogies

Paul Stewart and Chris Riddell's elaborate universe in *The Edge Chronicles* simply demands to have more tales told of it. Trilogies mirror the beginning-middle-end of a

single story structure, but on a bigger scale. The first book sets
the scene, introduces the main characters, shows them in action,
solving some smaller dilemma, but ends with the suggestion of
bigger problems still unresolved.

③ Different perspectives

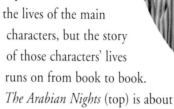

You may be bursting to tell the story of one of the
minor characters from your finished story. This is
another way of writing a sequel. In *A Series of
Unfortunate Events* (left) each book
is a separate adventure in
the lives of the main
characters, but the story
of those characters' lives
runs on from book to book.
The Arabian Nights (top) is about
Scheherazade who told Sultan Schariar a new story every night
for a thousand and one nights because her life depended on
it. Each story stopped on a cliff-hanger, as a new one grew
out of it. In the end the Sultan was so hooked on
Scheherazade's stories, he cancelled
his decree to execute her and let
her live.

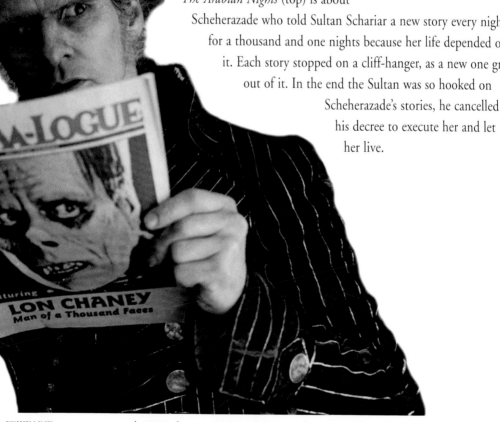

back story – the history of people or events that happened before the actual story begins

chapter synopsis – an outline description saying briefly what happens in each chapter

cliffhanger – ending a chapter or switching viewpoint stories at a nail-biting moment

dramatic irony – the reader knows something the characters don't; it could be scary!

editing – removing all unnecessary words from your story and making it the best shape it can be

editor – the person who works in a publishing house and finds new books to publish. They also advise authors on how to improve their storytelling methods by telling them what needs adding or cutting

first person viewpoint – a viewpoint that allows a single character to tell the story as if they had written it. The reader feels as if that character is talking directly to them, e.g. 'It was July when I left for Timbuctu. Just the thought of going back there made my heart sing.'

foreshadowing – dropping hints of coming events or dangers that are essential to the outcome of the story

genre – a particular type of fiction, e.g. fantasy, historical, adventure, science fiction are all examples of different genres

internal critic – the voice that constantly picks holes in your work and makes you want to give up writing

list – the list of book titles that a publisher has already published or is about to publish

manuscript – your story when it is written down, either typed or by hand

metaphor – calling a man 'a mouse' is a metaphor. It is a word picture. From it we learn in one word that the man is timid or pathetic, not that he is actually a mouse

motivation – the reason why a character does something

narrative – the telling of the story or sometimes meaning the story itself

omniscient viewpoint – the all-seeing eye which sees all the characters and tells readers how they are acting and feeling

plagiarism – copying someone else's work and passing it off as your own; it is a serious offence

plot – the sequence of events that drive a story forwards; the problems that the hero must resolve

point of view (POV) – the eyes through which a story is told

publisher – a person or company who pays for an author's manuscript to be printed as a book and who distributes and sells that book

sequel – a story that carries an existing one forward

simile – saying something is like something else. It is a word picture e.g. clouds liked frayed lace

synopsis – a short summary that describes what a story is about and introduces the main characters

theme – the main issue that the story addresses, e.g. good versus evil, how power corrupts, the importance of truth etc a story can have more than one theme

third person viewpoint – a viewpoint that describes the events of the story through a single character's eyes, e.g. 'Jem's heart leapt in his throat. He'd been dreading this moment for months.'

unsolicited submission – sending a book or story to a publisher without their asking you to. These submissions usually end up in 'the slush pile'

writer's block – when writers think they can no longer write, or have used up all their ideas

Most well-known writers have their own websites. They will give you lots of information about their own books, and many will give you hints and advice about writing too. Try Brian Jacques' www.redwall.org.

The Listen and Write site on the BBC website is all about writing poetry, but there are lots of fun exercises with rap, similes and freeform verse that will make all your written words sparkle: www.bbc.co.uk/education/listenandwrite/home.htm

Ask for a subscription to magazines such as *Cricket* and *Cicada* for your birthday. Or find them in your library. They publish the very best in young people's short fiction and you can learn your craft and read great stories at the same time. *Cicada* also accepts submissions from its subscribers. www.cricketmag.com

Make a good friend of your local librarian. They can direct you to useful sources of information that you might not have thought of. They will also know of any published author scheduled to speak in your area.

Get your teacher to invite a favourite author to speak at your school.

Places to submit your stories

The magazine *Stone Soup* which accepts stories and artwork from 8- to 13-year-olds. Their website is www.stonesoup.com

The Young Writers Club – an Internet-based club where you can post your stories. Check them out at: www.cs.bilkent.edu.tr/~david/derya/ywc.html. Or *Potluck Children's Literary Magazine* at members.aol.com/potluckmagazine

Young Writer at www.mystworld.com/youngwriter and other similar sites at www.kidauthors.com for 6- to 18-year-olds.

www.kidpub.org/kidpub – a subscription club that posts 40,000 young people's stories 'from all over the planet'.

Writing links on Kids on the Net: kotn.ntu.ac.uk/creative/links.htm and Google's Young Writers' Resource Directory: directory.google.com/Top/Arts/Writers_Resources/Young_Writers/

Works quoted/referred to in the text:

A Wizard of Earthsea, Ursula K. Le Guin, Puffin Books

Alice's Adventures in Wonderland, Lewis Carroll, Parragon

The Amazing Maurice and his Educated Rodents, Terry Pratchett, Corgi Books

Artemis Fowl, Eoin Colfer, Puffin

Arthur: The Seeing Stone, Kevin Crossley-Holland, Orion

The Bad Beginnings, A Series of Unfortunate Events, Lemony Snicket, Egmont

Beyond the Deepwoods, Edge Chronicles, Paul Stewart and Chris Riddell, Doubleday

The BFG, Roald Dahl, Puffin

The Curse of the Gloamglozer, Edge Chronicles, Paul Stewart and Chris Riddell, Doubleday

The Dream Master, Theresa Breslin, Corgi

The Earthsea Trilogy, Ursula K. Le Guin, Penguin

Eragon, Christopher Paolini, Corgi

The Hobbit, J.R.R. Tolkien, Collins

The Haunting of Hiram, Eva Ibbotson, Macmillan Children's Books

Harry Potter and the Philosopher's Stone, J.K. Rowling, Bloomsbury

Johnny and the Dead, Johnny Maxwell Trilogy, Terry Pratchett, Corgi Books

Krindlekrax, Philip Ridley, Puffin

The Legend of Luke, The Redwall Series, Brian Jacques, Random House Red Fox

The Lion, the Witch and the Wardrobe, C. S. Lewis, Collins

The Lord of the Rings, J. R. R. Tolkien, George Allen & Unwin

The Moon of Gomrath, Alan Garner, Armada Lions Collins

Northern Lights, Philip Pullman, Scholastic

Peter Pan, J. M. Barrie, Hodder Children's Books

The Phantom Tollbooth, Norton Juster, Collins

The Snow Queen, Hans Christian Andersen, translated by L.W. Kingsland, Oxford University Press

The Stones are Hatching, Geraldine McCaughrean, Oxford University Press

The Tale of Despereaux, Kate DiCamillo, Walker Books

The Weirdstone of Brisingamen, Alan Garner, Armada Lions Collins

The Wide Window, A Series of Unfortunate Events, Lemony Snicket, Egmont

The Wings of a Falcon, Cynthia Voigt, Harper Collins Lions

The Wizard of Oz, L. Frank Baum, Simon and Schuster

Picture Credits: Alamy: 38 all, 45t, 46t, 56t, 57b, Art Archive: 7t, 9t, 19b, 20t, Bridgeman Art Library: 22r, 48t. Corbis RF: 6t, 7b, 8l, 8-9c, 9r, 12-13 all, 15 all, 17 all, 20b, 29t, 32t, 39r, 48-49c, 49t, 51 all, 54-55 all, 62t, 63b. Creatas: 1, 3, 4t, 14t, 18t, 30t, 34t, 36t, 40 all, 42-43 all, 44t, 50t, 50-51t, 56 all, 57t, 58-59c, 59b, Dickens House Museum: 14c. Rex Features: 5t, 10-11 all, 16 all, 18-19 c, 21b, 23b, 24-25 all, 26t, 26-27c, 27r, 28t, 28-29c, 30-31c, 32b, 33r, 34b, 35t, 36-37c, 37t, 38-39c, 41 all, 44b, 47t, 49r, 58t, 60-61.